**Complete
Book Launch
Action Plan
Included!**

BOOK

Marketing Checklist
for Self-Publishing

J. Bruce Jones

BruceTheBookGuy.com

Book Marketing Checklist for Self-Publishing
Complete Book Launch Action Plan Included!

By J. Bruce Jones

Published by Bruce Jones Design Inc
781-255-7171 • http://www.BruceTheBookGuy.com

Amazon Author Central Page
http://www.amazon.com/author/jbrucejones

Table of Contents

3 Simple Things I Would Do to Market My Book

1. Build a media kit that you can use for promotion, include in it:

   - Cover shots of your book, 6" wide, 4" and 2", 72 dpi and 300 dpi

   - Head shots of you holding the book next to your head, 6", 4" 2". Tie your book to you, you are one and the same.

   - Book description, 50 words, 150 words and 500 words, include title, author, description, website and where you can get it.

   - Author description, 50 word, 150 word, and 500 word, be sure to include your book title, website and where you can buy the book.

   With this simple media kit you are ready for promotion, social media, and interviews.

2. I hope you have a blog or web presence, put a page about your book on the blog. Include a cover shot, specs, book and author descriptions, quotes, links to where someone can buy the book.

   Google's Blogger blogs are an excellent place to start for an author website. They are free, easy to set up and change, will handle all kinds of media and are part of the Google network. Google likes their own.

3. Blog your book, page by page or paragraph by paragraph. The entire book, add good titles on each post. Have a description line at the bottom, which includes author name, book title and link to where you can buy it. On the side of the blog or site have a thumbnail cover image with the words Buy at Amazon under it and link to the sales page on Amazon.

• PART 1 •

BOOK
Marketing
Checklist

General Book Marketing Concepts

One of the most common questions I get asked by new authors is "What's Next?" They have pushed the published button and launched their book on Amazon.com and then go what do I do now? Books don't market themselves just because you are on Amazon. You need to be involved on a regular basis with getting your book out to the world and getting people to buy it. This is true wither you are an indie author or you have a publishing company behind you. Books need to be marketed in order to find customers. This book is about many of the tasks that you will need to do to launch and have a successfully selling book.

Who am I, my name is J. Bruce Jones and I am the author and creator of over 40 of my own books, many of them best sellers at different times and the graphic designer for many more. I am a huge fan of self-publishing, I love it. We live in an amazing moment in time where we can publish, manufacture, distribute and sell our own ideas in book, video or audio form to the world. In this book I will layout and share with you what I have learned from the past number of years from my own book making and marketing efforts. Most of the ideas in this book are directed to indie and self-publishers but they will also work with books published by traditional houses.

I will be talking about books that are published as paperback using the print-on-demand side of Amazon, called CreateSpace.com and also the e-book side using the Kindle platform. There are many ways to publish your book but for success you will need to market and that is what this book is about. This book is set up in a checklist format that you can use to set up your own marketing.

So lets get started with some general concepts and ideas about book marketing.

- Your book marketing begins the day you start writing your book. We often don't even know we are starting a book project, but we need to start building out our author platform as soon as you can. Your author platform are all the ways that your readers and fans are connected to you. We will be talking more about this shortly.

- Amazon doesn't do your online marketing for you. You have to market your book.

- It is important to build some kind of central web home for your book, this can be a website or a blog. Facebook and Twitter are not homes for your book. You want to have a place online that you can blog from, host content, collect email names, have your bio and your book description and info, and have connections so readers can buy.

- Build a web site around your own content and sponsor your site with your own books.

- Build your author platform!

- Build out your marketing wheel. Have a central home where all your social media and other properties can point to. From this home have a clear path for buying your book.

- Give Away to Get. Give away sample chapters, maybe even full books, related content, and information. Deliver however your reader wants. Fans need to touch and feel your content.

- Web Traffic Matters, only about 1% of visitors will buy, but you need to bring in the other 99% to get those one. Be out there, be public and bring in readers.

- Build a mixture of online and off-line marketing.

- Book marketing is a continual process, do something everyday.

- Publishing on Amazon is important, start here first then branch out.

- Amazon book reviews are important, ask your readers to add a book review to your book.

- Have the best cover you can afford,

- Edit, Copy Edit and Proof Read, pay an editor to clean up your book. It is one of the most important things you can do.

- Good healthy book descriptions are important, use all the space they give you. Books are found by words in Google and Amazon search but only if the words are there to be found.

- Your Table of Contents are your book's benefits, don't do Chapter 1, Chapter 2, be descriptive in your list of chapters.

- Try not to end up with a garage full of books, use print-on-demand and e-books. Keep your costs to a minimum. You can always print later.

- If you think you are going to be selling your book in stores be sure to buy your own ISBN number, also look at IngramSpark.com instead of CreateSpace.

- Create an event around the release of your book. Build some buzz about it using all of the tools available.

- You don't need to advertise in traditional media to have a successful book.

How to Market Your Book Video Training
Learn more about marketing your book,
in my video training course.

http://bruce-the-book-guy.usefedora.com/courses/how-to-market-your-book

Start Marketing Your Book the Day You Start Writing

Ideally marketing your book starts the day you start writing it. We often don't even know we are writing a book when we start assembling content. But the key is to start reaching out to the world with your ideas as soon as you can. For most people this is a hard concept to get our heads around. We don't know what we are writing and we often don't want to release anything until we feel it is perfect. But to gain exposure and to start building our author platform we need to start releasing content as early as possible. It doesn't have to be perfect. In fact it most likely will not be. But it takes a while for the world to find us and connect with us. If we start releasing our ideas and content Google will notice and start sending people our way if we give them a place to send fans to. The goal is to build an audience of fans who know and like us and who are there when we release our books.

____ Work on building out your author platform.

Your author platform are all the ways that people connect with you. Some are just loose social media connections, some are stronger and are on your email lists and the strongest are actual buyers of your stuff. But they are all the people that can potentially buy your book.

Start Your Platform

____ Begin building an author website or blog

____ Begin building your email list of interested fans

____ Register an author URL for your website, NameNameAuthor.com will work if you can't get your name

____ Set up your social media sites, Facebook, Pinterest, Instagram, Linkedin, Twitter, YouTube and any others that you think your fans will be at. You want to be in their world.

Connecting with Influencers

____ Research bloggers and people who have influence in your market

____ Connect with these people using social media, Google+, Twitter, Facebook, Linkedin, their YouTube Channel, Pinterest, Periscope, etc.

____ Subscribe to their blogs, Facebook, Linkedin groups and email lists

____ Start commenting and engaging with them on their blogs and social media sites. Try to get on these people's radar, start building a relationship. This will become much more important when we come to launching your book.

Social Media Homes

____ Build an Open Facebook group around your topic, you can also do a Fan page, this can be a very powerful tool.

____ Build social media locations for you or your book, Twitter, Pinterest, Google+, Linkedin, Snapchat, Instagram and YouTube. Pick a couple to get started.

Offline Connections

____ Connect now for the future with local bookstores, coffee shops, and other outlets where you can sell your books. Depending on what your topic is there are many non-traditional places to sell also. Retail stores, professional services, speaking, conferences, etc.

_____ Build a list of local media, TV, radio, and print that you can connect with. Connect with their social media sites, start to get on their radar. ID who the personalities are and connect with them.

_____ As you get close to publishing your book pull together your Book Media Kit. Write your author bio and book descriptions. Collect cover images, bio images, videos, everything we will use to launch your book.

_____ Start building out your author/book website with all of this content. Have it ready to go for when you publish your book, collect email names.

_____ You should be putting up regular posts related to the book as you work on the writing. These can be story lines, sample sections, describing the writing and publishing process, images and related content. These posts will be used to build interest, Google search traffic, and for building up your mailing list. Be sure to follow the Kindle Select rules on duplicate content if you are going to use this Amazon program, see below.

Resources

Register your website url with companies like DirectNic.com, GoDaddy.com, or Hostgator.com

Build out your website using blogging platforms like WordPress or Google Blogger. Or web site builders like, Wix.com, Weebly.com, and SquareSpace.com. There are many available these are just a few.

How to Market Your Book Video Training
Learn more about marketing your book,
in my video training course.

http://bruce-the-book-guy.usefedora.com/courses/how-to-market-your-book

---

Selling on Amazon

Amazon.com is most likely where you will be selling your book. This site is one of the best book and product research tools ever invented. They tell you tons of information about your market, your readers, what they like and don't like if you spend some time checking it out. By using what you learn you can adjust your book to key into your readers wants and needs. Marketing isn't just pushing out lots of info about your book it is also making sure your book answers the key problems that your market has.

Make Your Book Work on the Amazon Sales Page

_____ A good cover that is easy to read as a thumbnail, remember we see most of our books now as thumbnail images from Amazon searches. Can readers figure out what your book is about when it is 1.5 inches high.

_____ A good title and subtitle, is it descriptive and works with search.

_____ A good healthy book description. Incorporate your categories, keywords and the main points about your book into the description. Drop in your Table of Contents. Many authors don't do this. Remember books are found with search, can yours be found.

_____ Publish both Kindle and CreateSpace paperback versions. If you have time produce an audio version. Give your readers every format.

_____ Link your website with a book cover thumbnail image to your Amazon sales page, make it an affiliate link.

___ Use the social media links from the Amazon sales page

___ Email Amazon with your book categories for the international Amazon sites.

___ Set up your Amazon affiliate account, use this link for your website and any posts about your book. Gives you a little extra juice.

___ Use the Amazon social medial affiliate Facebook and Twitter links. Post regularly.

___ Ask for book reviews. Book reviews are a big part of having success on Amazon

Amazon Author Central

___ Filled out Amazon Author Central page, bio, images, videos, link your blog, Every author is eligible for the free Central site, be sure to use it.

___ Link all your books to your Author Central page.

___ Your Author Central Bio is also your Kindle bio, make sure your have one.

___ Add your Author Central web address to your book's front matter and on your website. This can be a live link in your Kindle book.

___ Sign up on the international Amazon Author Central pages.

Kindle Select and Lending Programs

___ Kindle Select Program is a program offered by Amazon for Kindle books. If you are willing to give Kindle exclusivity of your book for a 90 day period they will let you price your book for free for a mix of 5 days during the 90. A lot of authors use the program to help jumpstart their book sales. You can only use this program if you don't have any of the book content anywhere on the web. Not posting any content is a decision you will need to make when you are starting your marketing. Many authors have found pretty good success with this program. You are only limited for 90 days and then you have to renew.

Personally I am a big fan of posting your content on your website as soon as you can to start getting exposure to Google and your fans but not everyone agrees on this. The Select Program doesn't apply to physical paperback books. You can read more about this program when you upload your book on the Kindle KDP site.

___ I always sign up for the Kindle Lending program. You often make more money lending your book than you do selling your book.

Kindle Select and Lending program along with several other options are located on the Kindle upload pages.

Resources

- Amazon Author Central, https://authorcentral.amazon.com/
- Amazon Affiliate, https://affiliate-program.amazon.com/
- Kindle Select program, https://kdp.amazon.com/select

How to Market Your Book Video Training
Learn more about marketing your book,
in my video training course.

http://bruce-the-book-guy.usefedora.com/courses/how-to-market-your-book

---

Book Launch Prep & Building Out Your Media Kit

There are lots of ways to launch your book, but one of the ways that is often overlooked is having a library of marketing materials at hand. These can be used for your website, social media, for interviews, and the local press. The best time to make these are just as you are releasing your book. This is usually when you still have access to your book and/ or cover designer and can have them give you the pieces.

Graphics

___ Produce some book cover promo photos made in 3 sizes 6" wide, 4" wide, 2" wide, rgb, at 72 and 300dpi. Request these from your cover designer, make them part of the design requirements.

___ Find a local photographer and produce some promo headshots.

___ Be sure to have some promo headshots with your book cover.

Promo Videos

___ Prepare a book announcement video, include a call to action at the end.

___ Prepare a book trailer video, include a call to action at the end.

___ Upload the trailer and announcement videos to YouTube, include a good title, live http web links, good healthy descriptions and keywords. Also include a short bio and your social media information.

_____ Connect your videos to all social media sites using the share and embed buttons. These can also be uploaded to your Amazon Author Central page.

Book Website and Social Media

_____ Build out your book media page on your website.

_____ Choose keywords and hashtags on your book topic for social media.

_____ Put an ad graphic for your book on your site, link it to the Amazon sales page. Use the 2" thumbnail image from your kit for the book graphic. Make it an affiliate link if possible.

_____ Produce an author One Sheet pdf book info sheet with author bio and contact info.

_____ Produce a free pdf sample chapter that you can email out and attach to your site. Add any related graphics, attached your One Sheet to the back.

_____ Continue to post in your Facebook Group, Blog and various Social Media sites.

_____ Pull together some kind of free gift, a pdf report, some short videos, an email series that you can use as a bonus for buying the book. This is called a lead magnet, it is a thank you for signing up. Direct people to sign-up on your list to receive this content after they have bought the book. One of the fields in your email sign-up form is for the book receipt number. Your buyer list is a great list to gather. These are people who will spend mony on your products.

Announcements

____ Write and edit your press releases.

____ Prepare your launch announcement or any articles that you might be releasing to your Blogger and Influencers network.

____ Put together a virtual book tour with your Blogging network. Have articles and posts ready to go when you launch. These relationships need to be built over time so that these people will post for you.

____ Record some interviews for your website and marketing using Skype or Zoom.com.

____ Making a book announcement video.

____ Fill out Amazon Author Central page once your book is live.

____ Link to your Amazon Author Central Page.

Key Elements in an Author Media Kit

Your Author Media Kit is an essential part of your author/book website and your marketing. It has all the elements that you need to promote your book. Not only is it for building up the elements that you will need to send out like promo book covers and such. But it also has the resources that fans, the press and anyone else needs to be able to download when they are promoting you.

Author Bio
Have several different length bios for different uses
- A very short bio you can use at the end of a blog post, remember to include your web address.

- 50-100 word bio

- 250-500 word bio

2" wide

4" wide

6" wide

Author Photos

Spend a little money and have a professional photo done. Also be sure to have some images done with you holding your book up near your head. Have several different sizes produced, 300dpi for print uses and 72dpi for web use. I would also have some larger ones and also a thumbnail size. I like a 2", 4" and 6" image in both 300dpi and 72dpi. A head shot with and without your book.

Book Photos

Same as the author pictures a 2", 4" and 6" image in both 300dpi and 72dpi. Be sure to ask your book cover designer for these images. **(Make this part of the original book cover project.)**

Any awards, testimonials and reviews. Have a running Word document where you save these.

Contact Details

Phone, email, Skype, website addres, social media addresses

Interview Questions

Sample interview questions, these can be very helpful for the interviewer.

Social Media Links
All of your social media connections, YouTube, Facebook, Twitter, Pinterest, Instagram, etc.

Recent Speaking events, maybe a video or two if possible

Your Book Info
- Info about the book, specs, ISBN number, pages
- Book description
- Photo of the book, several sizes and resolutions, 300dpi and 72 dpi, including one with you holding the book
- Where to buy your book, print and ebook with links
- Book Reviews
- Sample chapter

Resources
Online photo editing sites
- Picnik.com http://www.picnik.com
- FotoFlexer.com http://fotoflexer.com/
- Lunapic.com http://www.lunapic.com/editor/
- Online-Converter http://www.online-convert.com/

How to Market Your Book Video Training
Learn more about marketing your book,
in my video training course.

http://bruce-the-book-guy.usefedora.com/courses/how-to-market-your-book

---

Preparing for Your Book Launch and General Marketing

The big day is here, your book is done, edited and ready for publishing. To give your book a great start you want to conduct a book launch instead of just releasing it. Book launches can be very involved and take a lot of planning. Or you can work with what you have. The key here is to work with whatever author platform you have put together and with all other media you have access to. With a little thinking and planning you can have a successful book launch.

____ Book is written, and edited.

____ Book is designed, formatted, copyedited and proof read before publishing.

____ Book is uploaded to your publishing sites (Kindle, CreateSpace/ Amazon, others, etc.) and ready to go.

____ Research best selling books in your subject matter and be sure to incorporate their categories into your book's description and keywords.

____ Select your book categories, 1 for Createspace, 2 for Kindle. Categories should be related to your book subject matter to help with positioning and proper ranking. Select categories that have a low number of books in them and try not to have a super star author at the top.

____ Pricing, I put pricing after you have looked at the other books in your category and reviewed the best selling books.

E-Book Kindle, $.99 to $2.99, they can be more, look at the two royalty settings, 35% and 70%. For the launch most authors price their books at $.99 and then increase it after a couple of weeks.

Print paperback books, look at competition, size, market, what the market will bear. I tend to price my 8.5" x 11" books around $9.95 for black an white and $14.95 for color. My 6" x 9" books are often in the $6.95-$7.95 range. These are rough ranges. Number of pages, size, color all matter when figuring out your price. I often try to generate around $2.50-$3.50 for my royalty payment, if that helps. Again there are no hard rules on this.

Launch

____ Hopefully you have been building a relationship with your bloggers and influencers. Let them know the launch date.

____ Ask them to give you their support.

____ Send your influencers a free book or at least a pdf of your book, you can also send it as an Amazon gift.

____ Ask for an interview from your influencers, getting a review or possibly publish an article you wrote around a topic that relates to your book. These relationships need to be nurtured over time, don't just show up demanding that they publish your stuff.

____ Prepare your platform and email lists for an announcement blast about your upcoming book. Build anticipation for your book.

____ Start announcing your upcoming book release date on your social media platforms.

____ Ask people to buy your book on a specific day and ask for reviews.

____ The day you release ask your fans to support your book.

____ If on Kindle reduce your book price to $.99.

____ Publish your book on Amazon.com Congratulations!

____ Buy your book so you know everything is working, this starts your Amazon ranking. I like to do this several days before you actually release your book. The key here is to have it already live so you know everything is working.

____ Have several friends buy your book and submit reviews. Amazon reviews need to come from actual paying customers. Don't announce that the book is ready for buying yet but you want to know everything is working and you have some reviews.

____ Take screen shots of your book's Amazon rank as it moves into best seller status. This information is located in the Product Details area on your Amazon Book Page. Best seller status is generally regarded for books that reach into the top 100 ranking in their categories.

Best Seller

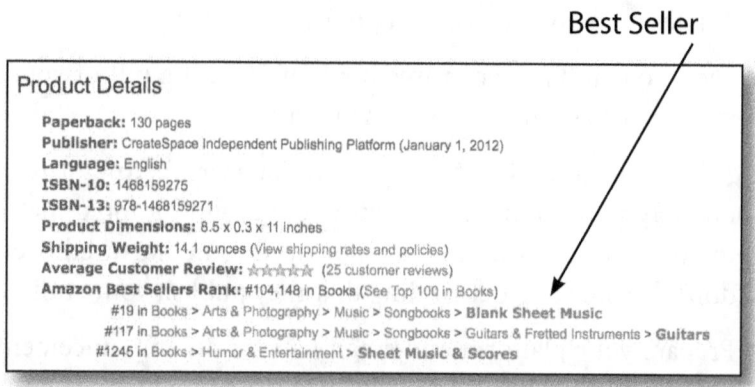

Amazon Book Product Details, located on the Amazon book sales page, about half way down.

Going for Best seller Status

The theory for producing a best selling book is to drive as many people as you can to buy your book through the narrowest time frame in a book category that doesn't have very many books in it. You also want to pick a category that doesn't have a popular best selling author or big selling book at the top that you have to take on.

This is why building your platform is important; you need fans to do this. If you can do this it is very likely that you can create a bestselling book. Maybe even a #1 category best seller. It won't last long so be sure to screen capture the Products Details area of the Amazon sales page for your marketing. Generally this technique works best with Kindle books because you can lower the price down to $.99. But I have also seen it work with paperback books but the per book price will by much higher.

____ Research your categories.

____ Select specific categories that have under 5-7000 books in them, better if you can find one with low thousands or even hundreds of books.

____ Try to find a category that doesn't have books in the top 2,000 overall sales rank.

____ When you upload your book, select the BASAC book categories as close as you can to the Amazon categories. Be sure to include the Amazon categories in your description and keywords.

Launch Your Book

____ Prepare and send out your launch announcement or any articles that you might be releasing to your Blog and Influencers network.

____ Send press releases out to PR sites, free and paid.

____ Email your list that you are launching your book and would love to have their support. Give them the book link and instructions on when to buy.

____ Lower your Kindle price to $.99.

____ If released over Createspace lower your price.

____ Announce the upcoming release through all your social media

____ Release your book.

____ Email your list that your book is now live.

____ Announce your book is live on your social media sites, include a cover shot and the link to Amazon.com.

____ If you are giving away a free bonus gift tell everyone how to get it.

One of the questions I am asked is can you get the email addresses and names of your book buyers. The answer is no, Amazon doesn't reveal this information. But there is a way to get some of the names using a technique call the Amazon Receipt Strategy. Remember your buyer is your most valuable connection, this is someone that actually put down money and bought your product. You want to be connected to this person.

____ Conduct a Virtual Launch Party on Google Hangout.

____ Release your Virtual Book launch and tour.

____ Post your progress in your social media accounts during the launch day about what is going on, how exciting it is. Encourage others to join in, get your fans involved to get you over the top to a #1 position.

_____ Be sure to screen capture your Amazon ranking as you climb, don't try to guess the top, just keep recording the screen during the day. This information is located in the Product Details section of your Amazon book sales page.

_____ Re-email your list about your launch, be sure to not burn out this list.

Amazon Receipt Strategy

- First you need to pull together a bonus gift for buying your book, a pdf report, a short video series, extra training, something you can give away. This is a great way to develop a list of your buyers.

- Second instruct your readers to sign-up on a email sign-up form on our website using their book receipt number to gain access. There are a variety of services that you can use for this. I use AWeber.com

- Third send them a link to the offer or whatever the gift is. You now have their email address and often their name.

How to Market Your Book Video Training
Learn more about marketing your book,
in my video training course.

http://bruce-the-book-guy.usefedora.com/courses/how-to-market-your-book

---

Online, General Book Marketing

Promoting your book is something that you need to do continually over a long period of time through a lot of different channels. There isn't one specific method or way to do it. The goal here is to be continually marketing your book. This chapter contains a variety of different ideas that you can do. We start with having your media kit ready if you are connecting with a podcaster or blogger. Media outlets need cover shots, bios, descriptions and more. You want these ready to go.

We all have some kind of phone, usually with the ability to record audio and video.Once your media kit is ready then start building some video and audio content that you can use to spread your message.

One of the things that we tend to forget is that we have a lot of electronic fingers out into the world. We have bios, online listings, signatures all kinds of stuff. We need to keep these updated with out latest bios and accomplishments including our book. And remember to give clear links to your Amazon sales page.

____ Produce some promo book cover photos made in 3 sizes for each book, 6", 4", and 2", rgb format, at 72dpi and 300dpi which you will use for print applications.

Same specs for the headshots also. If you are giving a talk they will want a head shot and book shot for promoting the event.

____ Promo headshots.

____ Promo headshots with book cover.

____ Produce several book announcement videos, very easy to producte with a smart phone. Host these on YouTube and then share across your social media platforms.

____ Produce several book trailer videos.

____ Continue to make videos around your book topic.

____ Connect videos to all social media sites. Be sure to have healthy video description with live http:// links and calls to action.

____ Press releases written and edited.

____ Press releases sent out to PR sites, free and paid.

____ Build your book media page on your website or blog.

____ Put an ad graphic for your book on your site, link it to the Amazon sales page.

____ Fill out Amazon Author Central page once your book is live.

____ Use the social media share buttons from your Amazon sales page.

____ Prepare a one page pdf book info sheet with author bio for the media or public speaking.

____ Post info about your book on your blog, about your subject, and about your activities. Take people on your journey.

____ Post regularly on your Social Media sites around your topic and book.

____ Interact with your fans in your Facebook group, social media and anywhere else, including YouTube, respond to all comments.

____ Be sure all your web and social media efforts are up to date, connected and can send interested readers to Amazon for buying.

____ Look for media outlets that will publish your press release or book reviews.

____ Ask for book reviews. Book reviews are a big part of having success on Amazon.

____ Kindle Select Program is a program offered by Amazon for Kindle books. If you are willing to give Kindle exclusivity of your book for a 90 day period they will let you price your book for free for a mix of 5 days during the 90. A lot of authors use the program to help jumpstart their book sales. You can only use this program if you don't have any of the book content anywhere on the web. Not posting your book content is a decision you will need to make when you are starting your marketing. Many authors have found pretty good success when they initial launch their book with this program.

Personally I am a big fan of posting your book content on your own website as soon as you can to start getting exposure but not everyone agrees on this. With Kindle Select you are only limited for 90 days and then you have to renew. Limiting your content doesn't apply to physical paperback books going through CreateSpace, you can do what you want. You can read more about this program when you upload your book on the Kindle KDP site.

____ Review all your online bios in social media, Linkedin, Facebook, industry groups for the most up to date info. Be sure to mention your book and where to get it or more information.

____ Update your email signature line about your book, include a link to Amazon.

____ Be sure to announce your book in any online groups or organizations that you might be part of.

Book Promo Sites

____ List your book in Goodreads and other online review sites.

____ There are lots of free and paid book promotion websites for you to list your book on for exposure. Some will work if you are using the KDP Select program. Be sure to read the terms of service and be aware of the rules around Kindle Select if you are using that Amazon program.

Resources

Kindle Select program, https://kdp.amazon.com/select
Goodreads, https://www.goodreads.com/

Making Your Book Trailer Video

How to Make a Video Book Trailer Using Your Smartphone
https://youtu.be/Gg13mwmL6js

Video should be part of your book marketing efforts. It is a powerful tool that you can use on your website, in your social media and on YouTube to promote your book. Below are some tips to help make your video effective. Your book trailer video should cover 4 basic topics and be 1 to 3 minutes long.

1. Who you are, your name.

2. What you have got, the name of the book.

3. What the book will do for you and what you will learn, use your Table of Contents to come up with your list of key points.

4. What you want the viewer to do next, buy your book on Amazon. com, go to your website, give them a call to action.

Smartphones work great for making nice simple, one take video book trailers. The quality is great and if you record in a quiet place the audio will be just fine. You can always improve but smartphones work very well for this purpose.

Key point for quality is to make your smartphone nice and stable, use a small tripod from Amazon.com or from a site like Caddiebuddy.com. Also turn off any radios or fans that might make extra noise.

Quick Tips

- Almost any simple digital camera will do for making a video. This includes the smart phone in your pocket. The quality is amazing and most are connected right to YouTube.

- A little tripod can really help with the quality.

- Don't have a camera, then use the Save as Movie option of PowerPoint or a screen capture program like Screenflow.com or Screenr.com.

- Keep the video short. This is key; around 1-3 minutes is perfect.

- If you can do it in one take, you might not need to do any editing. If you are editing, then make each shot at least 10 seconds; (count in your head). You can also add in still images, or video from a Power-Point presentation.

- Lighting is important. Turn on the lights or stand by a window. A dark video just doesn't look very good. Watch out for backlighting such as a window behind you. It can kill your video.

- Stay close to the camera for good sound, turn off any radios, and watch out for background noise. If your camera has a mic input, you can also add one for better quality, lavalier mics work well.

- In your video, give viewers a call-to-action: ask them to do something, call, go to a web site, suggest something to get them to your web site.

- Do some simple editing with iMovie on the Mac, MovieMaker on the PC, for more complex, use Premier. You can even edit right in You-Tube or the new YouTube Capture app that works for iPhone. Many cameras also come with video editing software.

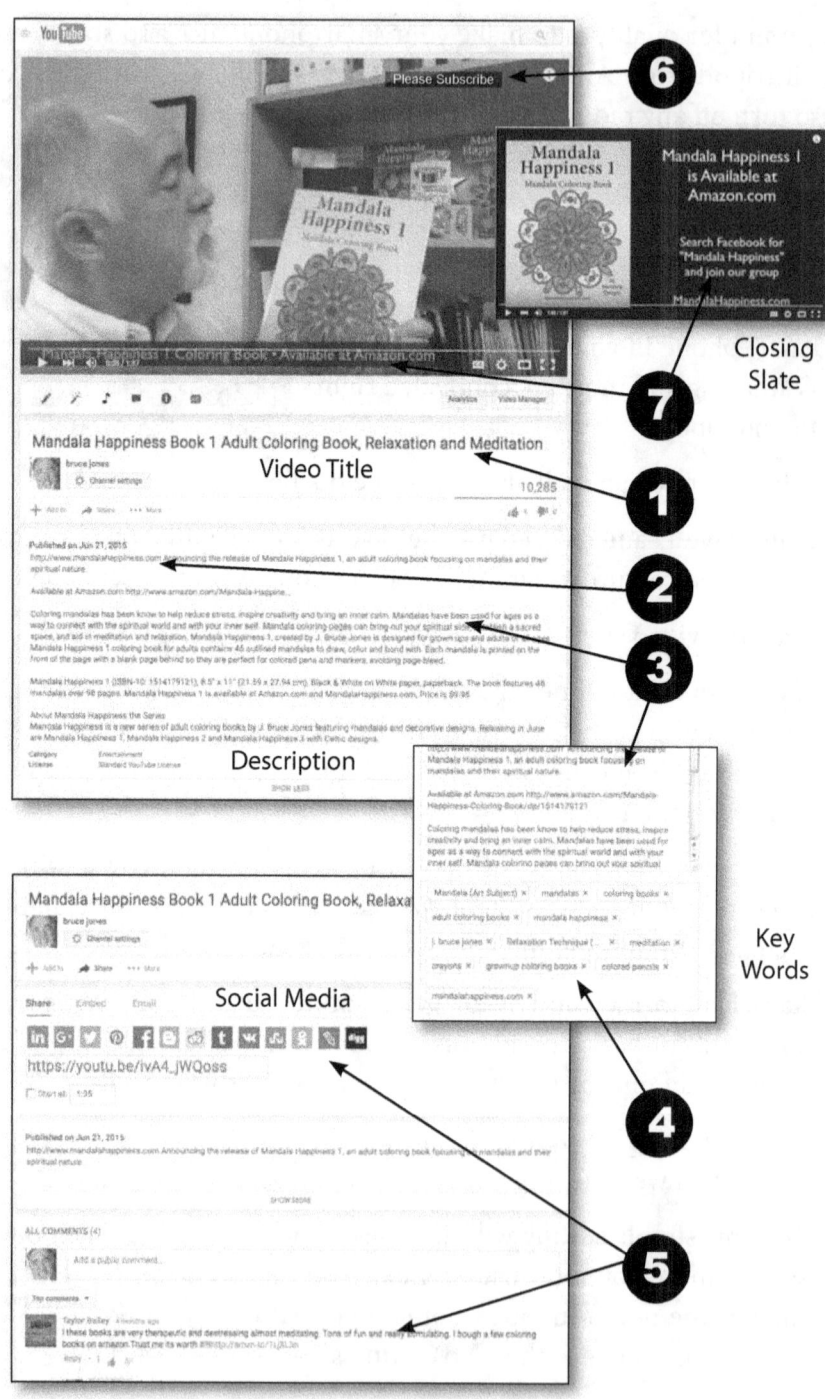

Closing Slate

Video Title

Description

Key Words

Social Media

- Add your web address along the bottom or lower third of the screen. Add contact info or a call-to-action at the end. Tell viewers that your book is available on Amazon.

- Upload your video to YouTube, then link it to a blog, your website, Facebook and other social media sites.

Setting Up Your Videos

The key to getting your videos found in YouTube and Google search is to fill in all the boxes YouTube provides with lots of relevant text when you upload your video. This includes the video title, description, web address and key words or tags.

1. **Video Title**, have a good descriptive video title, include your main keyword.

2. In the initial sentence of the description, include a **full web address** as the first item, including the http://, then a short intro description. The first sentence needs to grab because this is all you initially see below your video.

3. Add a **full description**, fill it out with a lot of relevant descriptive copy, maybe with a transcript of the video. Include your contact info. You can really fill this area up with text. Google indexes this area so it is important to also add your keywords into the copy.

4. **Add Keywords or Tags** that Relate to the video and the topic, this is super important.

5. **YouTube is a social media platform**, this means share your video on all your social media platforms and interacting with people who comment on your videos.

6. **Use Annotations** and YouTube Cards to connect with other videos, make additional comments or give information.

7. All videos should have some kind of **call-to-action** (CTA), including a web address or contact info during or at the end of the video.

Off Line Book Marketing

We spend so much time focusing on our online platforms that we forget that there is an entire world out there that isn't based around FaceBook and Twitter. All of it can be used to promote our book.

____ Be sure to announce your book in any groups or organizations that you might be part of. They usually have newsletters with What's New sections and are always looking for content.

____ If you send out any regular mailings such as a newsletter be sure to announce it and include a regular ad for the book.

____ Add a picture of your book to your business card. Your business card is your personal brochure, make sure your book is on it, including where people can buy the book.

____ Contact your regional print and TV media, they love local stories.

____ If you speak to audiences at conferences or organizations be sure to bring books and sell from the stage or the back of the room. The profit margin on this can be pretty high.

____ Use your book as a calling card for prospects or consulting. People love receiving books. You can bet your competitors aren't.

____ If you are trying to connect with a new client, try sending a free paperback copy of your book directly from Amazon using their gift program or use FedEx. With FedEx you can also include a cover letter. People love receiving free stuff, this is a great way to get noticed.

• PART 2 •

BOOK
Launch
Action Plan

3 Simple Things I Would Do to Market My Book

1. Build a media kit that you can use for promotion, include in it:

   - Cover shots of your book, 6" wide, 4" and 2", 72 dpi and 300 dpi

   - Head shots of you holding the book next to your head, 6", 4" 2". Tie your book to you, you are one and the same.

   - Book description, 50 words, 150 words and 500 words, include title, author, description, website and where you can get it.

   - Author description, 50 word, 150 word, and 500 word, be sure to include your book title, website and where you can buy the book.

   With this simple media kit you are ready for promotion, social media, and interviews.

2. I hope you have a blog or web presence, put a page about your book on the blog. Include a cover shot, specs, book and author descriptions, quotes, links to where someone can buy the book.

   Google's Blogger blogs are an excellent place to start for an author website. They are free, easy to set up and change, will handle all kinds of media and are part of the Google network. Google likes their own.

3. Blog your book, page by page or paragraph by paragraph. The entire book, add good titles on each post. Have a description line at the bottom, which includes author name, book title and link to where you can buy it. On the side of the blog or site have a thumbnail cover image with the words Buy at Amazon under it and link to the sales page on Amazon.

Book Marketing with 3 Levels of Engagement

In Part One of this book I broke down and wrote about specific steps that you can take to market your book. Each chapter gives you a checklist of tasks or ideas. Part 2 takes a different approach. One of the most common questions I get asked is "What Now?" what should I do, usually right after the author has published their book on Amazon. Most authors I meet aren't into being marketers, they just want to write and publish their book and then that is it. "It was hard enough writing the book, now I have to market, what is that all about?" I have broken Part Two down into three sections or levels.

Level 1. Is for authors that don't want to do anything. They don't want to spend money, they don't want to post or blog or make videos or contact podcasters or anything. They just want to hit the publish button and somehow the book sells itself. Level 1 are my recommendations for those folks. You would be surprised, these are most of the authors I meet.

Level 2. Is for authors that want to do a little more effort. They are willing to spend a little money and maybe set up a small website or Facebook book page. They are also willing to turn their smart phone on and speak into it to make an announcement video.

Level 3. Authors who want to go full on. They have been building a platform, building an email list, willing to make videos and share them on their author/book website. They will also take the time to set up and conduct a book launch.

Marketing is hard, it is a continual and time consuming process. One of the Internet marketing leaders that I follow, Pamela Hendrickson recommends an 80/20 rule. Spend 80% of your time marketing your book; the writing was the 20% part. I know it took a lot of effort to write your book, sometimes years, but unfortunately that was the beginning. Now comes the hard part of getting people to find, see and then spend money on your book. Each level below builds on the one before, read through the ideas, select what works for you and jump in.

For real simple take a look at page 4 for three simple things I would do to market my book.

What ever you do come over and join my How to Publish Your Book Facebook group and let us know what you are doing.

https://www.facebook.com/groups/HowToPublishYourBook/

Level 1. Marketing My Book with Little Effort and $0 Dollars

Marketing starts the day you start your writing.

Before Releasing

- Be sure your book is edited and has a final proof read, twice if possible. Nothing will create a bad review more than bad grammar and spelling.

- Create a good descriptive table of contents, these are your books main benefits. They are also very useful for the back cover.

- Research your title and subtitle, do your readers know what the book is about. Don't fall in love with your title, it might be wrong.

- Add your web or Amazon Author Central address on the title page. If you are making a Kindle book make it a live http link.

- Have a good, clear cover designed. Make sure the cover is readable at thumbnail size. This is the size we usually see when we do a search on Amazon. Elements: title, subtitle, author name, maybe a short quote, maybe benefits, good cover art.

- If releasing a paperback book have an effective back cover. Elements: title, description, maybe a quote, benefits (Could be your Table of Contents), author picture, author bio, contact info, room for ISBN number.

- Promote your next book in the back of your current book. Drop in the first chapter of the next book, add your bio, how about yours services or that you speak and how to contact you.

- Set up your social media accounts, Facebook, YouTube, Google+, Pinterest, Linkedin, Instagram, Slideshare, SnapChat, Twitter, etc

- Start releasing content around your subject and from your book as early as you can. Pick 1-3 sites to focus on.

Releasing/Launch

- Pre-announce that you have a book coming out on your social media platforms. If you have other mailing lists then pre-announce on those also.

- Announce a release date for your book on your social media. Picking a date really helps give you focus.

- Announce the book release on your social media platforms with live links to the Amazon sales page.

- Update all bios on your social media sites with your current book information; include links to Amazon for your book if possible.

- Fill out your Amazon Author Central Account.

- Link your book to your Author Central Page.

- Take advantage of what Kindle and CreateSpace.com offers for programs.

Build a Media Kit

- Build a basic media kit for promotion and interviews, this can be on your computer or your website,

- Make up jpg book cover images in 3 sizes for marketing and posting, 2", 4" and 6", 300 dpi and 72 dpi. Your cover designer can give you these, make it part of the cover project.

- Make up a picture of yourself holding your book cover, preferable near your head, this can be as simple as a selfie.

- Prepare 50, 150-200 and 500 word bios and book descriptions with details you can have ready for promotion, interviews, blog posts.

After Releasing

- Use the Amazon sales page social media links to post about your book.

- Ask for Amazon reviews in your posts.

- Write and send out a press release on several of the free or paid PR sites.

- Add your book title and link to your email signature line.

- Let every company, organization, or association you are part of know about your new book, especially if they have a newsletter.

Level 2. I Can Go a Little Bigger and Make a Little More Effort

Include everything above

Before Releasing

- Register a URL for your name.
- Build an author blog or website, you can do this on Google's Blogger platform, it is free.
- Create your One Sheet, post on your website. This is your resume but more sales focused.
- Register with an email marketing service like AWeber, Mail Chimp or similar, start building an email list of fans and buyers.
- Add an email sign up box on your blog or website.
- Create a lead magnet from your book content and use it as a thank you gift for subscribers to your list, such as a sample chapter, a video series, pdf report, series of email auto-responder lessons.
- Work on building your author platform; bring these people into your mailing list.
- Research the main influencers in your market, make a master link.
- Build your Top 20 influencers and connect with them where they hang out.

- Build up a network of related blogs and websites that you can connect with and then use when it comes to launch time. Relationships need time and energy to build.

Releasing/Launch

- Build your online media kit for promotion and interviews.
- Conduct a simple book launch, pick a date and email your platform.
- Create a book announcement video and post it on YouTube, Facebook and your other social media platforms, including your author blog.
- Use a paid PR service like PRWeb and send out a press release for your book.
- Post on your social media accounts, Facebook, YouTube, Google+, Pinterest, Linkedin, be sure to link back to your website or blog. Actually be always doing this.

Build a Media Kit

- Build a media kit for promotion and interviews, this can be on your computer and your website.
- Make up jpg book cover images in 3 sizes for marketing and posting, 2", 4" and 6", 300 dpi and 72 dpi. Your cover designer can give you these.
- Make a promo picture of yourself holding your book cover, preferable near your head, also several without the book.
- Prepare 50, 150-200 and 500 word bios and book descriptions with details you can have ready for promotion, interviews, blog posts.

After Releasing

- Put a graphic of your book cover on your website and connect it to the book's Amazon sales page, use an affiliate link.

- Give away free pdf copies of your book for fans, reviews and press.

- Publish books on both Kindle and CreateSpace/Amazon

- Set up an Amazon affiliate account and post affiliated links to your website, Facebook and Twitter, really anywhere that you can

- Connect with local press and media for the local story.

- Build out a list of retail locations where you can speak and sell your book.

- Build out a list of potential speaking opportunities; start connecting with these people, organizations and locations.

How to Market Your Book Video Training
Learn more about marketing your book,
in my video training course.

http://bruce-the-book-guy.usefedora.com/courses/how-to-market-your-book

---

Level 3. I Want to Kick It Into Higher Gear, Try to Really Push It

Include everything above.

Before Releasing

- Build out your author platform further, more connections, more influencers, build your relationships. It is usually recommended to start build your platform of influencers at least 6 months before you launch your book.

- Continue to build out your author blog or website, more content, more posts. This continues on in all stages.

- Set up a Facebook open group around your topic.

- Make additional videos on subjects from your book, remember to have calls to action in your videos and include full descriptions with live http:// web links.

- Set up and conduct video interviews with sources from your book and industry leaders around your topic. Google Hangout, Zoom, and Skype can all work.

- Set up an editorial calendar for your posts, post regularly on your blog.

- Post regularly on your social media accounts, Facebook, YouTube, Google+, Pinterest, Linkedin, Twitter, and wherever your audience hangs out.

Releasing/Launch

- Do a full book launch and Amazon Best seller campaign accessing your platform and email list.

- It is time to access your Top 20 influencers that you have been building relationships with, conduct interviews, do guest blog posts on their blogs. Get their help when you do a book launch.

- Connect with the bloggers from Level 2 and conduct a virtual book tour with them.

- Use the Amazon Receipt strategy to build a list of buyers.

- Create a YouTube book trailer for your author blog or bookstore.

After Releasing

- Connect with your audience using Webinars and or Google Hangout.

- Speak at events.

- Create an audio version of your book.

- Repurpose your book into a course, coaching and consulting, workbooks, blog posts, video and podcast content, info graphics, reports, online learning, broken into a series of books, SlideShare.com presentations, email auto-responder series.

- Start on the next book.

Book Marketing Resources

Websites

50 Ways to Kickstart your Publicity from Molly Green Writer, blog. How to get your planning going for your book release
http://www.molly-greene.com/authors-50-fabulous-ways-to-kickstart-publicity/

71 Ways to Promote and Market Your Book, Kimberley Grabas put together this excellent set of tips on book marketing on her site YourWriterPlatform.com
http://www.yourwriterplatform.com/promote-and-market-your-book/

How to Build a Top Notch Media Kit from Molly Green Writer, blog, what are the media kit parts
http://www.molly-greene.com/how-to-build-a-media-kit/

How to Write a Killer Author Bio from Divrit.com blog
https://blog.dlvrit.com/2015/04/killer-blog-author-bio/

Some of my favorite writing and publishing resources
- **Write. Publish. Repeat. (The No-Luck-Required Guide to Self-Publishing Success),** by Sean Platt and Johnny B. Truant
- **61 Ways to Sell More Non-Fiction Kindle Books,** by Steve Scott
- **Kindle Publishing Package: How to Discover Best-Selling eBook Ideas + How to Write a Nonfiction eBook in 21 Days + 61 Ways to Sell More Nonfiction Kindle Books** by Steve Scott

- **Your First 1000 Copies: The Step-by-Step Guide to Marketing Your Book** by Tim Grahl
- **Book Launch Blueprint: The Step-by-Step Guide to Launching a Best seller** by Tim Grahl
- **Author Quick Guide to Making Your Book a Best Seller** by Kristen Eckstein
- **Don't Make Me Think, Revisited: A Common Sense Approach to Web Usability**, Steve Krug
- **Publish and Profit** by Mike Koenigs
- **How to Market a Book** by Joanna Penn
- **The Story Grid** by Steven Pressfield

I Also Follow These Authors/Teachers

- Nina Amir, http://howtoblogabook.com/
- Joan Stewart, http://publicityhound.com/
- Joel Friedlander, http://www.thebookdesigner.com/
- Pat Flynn, http://www.smartpassiveincome.com/

Book Formatting

- Building Your Book for Kindle for Mac by Amazon
- Building your Book for Kindle for the PC by Amazon
- From Word to Kindle by Aaron Shepard

Good Examples of Author Book Media Pages

Media page for Michael Stelzner's book launch
http://www.socialmediaexaminer.com/launch/media.html

Joanna Penn, from the Creative Penn, one of the top in this area
http://www.thecreativepenn.com/
Here is her media area http://www.thecreativepenn.com/contact/

Tim Ferriss, The Four Hour Work Week Guy
http://fourhourworkweek.com/overview/

Mardie Caldwell, has an excellent example of a interview questions pdf
http://www.mardiecaldwell.com/press-kit/

CJ Lyons, Thriller writer
http://cjlyons.net/contact/for-media/

Stephen R. Covey, 7 Habits of Highly Effective People, though
Dr. Covey has passed the site that promotes his books is set up very
well and is a good example.
https://www.stephencovey.com/

Laura Stack, The Productivity Pro
http://theproductivitypro.com/newsroom/

More Info on Building Your Author Media Site

Standout Books
https://www.standoutbooks.com/author-media-kit/

Tim Grahl
http://timgrahl.com/how-to-build-the-ultimate-author-website-in-1-hour/

30 Day Books
http://www.30daybooks.com/your-author-websites-media-page-14-items-to-include/

About J. Bruce Jones

I am a Massachusetts-based business graphic designer, author and musician. I am the author of more that 40 books. I write on all kinds of topics that interest me: business books on social media; and publishing, growing your business and increasing your visibility on YouTube; books on playing and writing music; geography textbooks for learning and coloring books for fun.

I am also the creator of the How to Publish Your Book School with courses on book publishing, Kindle, making children's books and marketing books. Learn more at http://bruce-the-book-guy.usefedora.com/

I will be continuing to write more books and produce videos on self-publishing, be sure to join my list so that you can follow and learn what I am doing at: http://www.BruceTheBookGuy.com

Also come over and join my How to Publish Your Book Facebook group and let me know about your projects. It is also a great place to ask me questions.
https://www.facebook.com/groups/HowToPublishYourBook/

I hope my book was helpful and gave you some great tips for your book publishing efforts. Reviews are really important for indie writers and I would really appreciate you leaving a review on Amazon

Thank you, Bruce

You've just published your first book. Now what? Learn how to market and sell it?

 I am here to help. In my new course I teach you everything I have learned about marketing and promoting over 40 of my own books. I will teach you the concepts and tools to successfully market and sell your book.

What Do I Get? This Course Includes

- General book marketing concepts, my main lessons
- Ideally book marketing begins the day we start writing our books. This video covers stuff to do before you release your book
- Amazon marketing, learn to use the most powerful store in the world to promote your book
- Preparing for your book launch, getting your fans, platform and the market ready.
- Everyone is trying to get an Amazon category best seller, Video 5 covers how.
- Video 6 walks you through how to set up your media kit.
- Your book is launched and on its way but the marketing doesn't really ever stop. In Video 7 I talk about what you can do on an ongoing basis.
- And finally we cover off-line marketing. Not everything is the web, this lesson covers things you can outside of the web.

Bonus Videos

A big part of my book marketing is building a home on the web where my fans can learn more about me and my books. A great way to do this is build an author/book blog or website. In two videos I show you how to build a book blog.

How to Market Your Book Video Training

http://bruce-the-book-guy.usefedora.com/courses/how-to-market-your-book